THE MULE

THE MULE

An Unexpected Ride

Author: Karen Rhea

XULON PRESS

Xulon Press
2301 Lucien Way #415
Maitland, FL 32751
407.339.4217
www.xulonpress.com

© 2020 by Karen Rhea

Unless otherwise indicated, Scripture quotations taken from the Holy Bible, New International Version (NIV). Copyright © 1973, 1978, 1984, 2011 by Biblica, Inc.™. Used by permission. All rights reserved.

Printed in the United States of America.

ISBN-13: 978-1-6312-9227-9

This book is dedicated to
William Joel Rhea.

Contents

Thoughts and Acknowledgements

Thank you, my friend and editor, Jennifer Burke for helping me write my story.

To my girlfriends, who are still with me and those who beat me to heaven; my encouragers, one and all.

My deep appreciation to my family, friends, acquaintances, and even strangers who find my life interesting.

Each of our lives is a treasure-trove of experiences to record and share. The importance of documenting our histories and significant life events become more urgent when loss occurs. My mother Gwen had dementia. My Uncle Bernard's mind was ravaged by Alzheimer's. I saw what the disease stole. Witnessing their growing struggle to communicate was heartbreaking. In their day, they were both great story-tellers. I wish their life experiences were in my library. Knowing nothing is to be taken for granted, I feel a deep contentment having this opportunity to share God's provision in my life.

Through the years, in social settings, friends encouraged me to detail my plunge over a cliff, and subsequent rescue by the indigenous people of Oaxaca, to their guests. To enhance the telling, I often wished I could produce photographs tucked in my album at home. Likewise, during speaking engagements, I lacked the ability to use Power-point. Therefore, my mind often wandered to a specific photograph that would have been ideal at that moment, visually portraying more than my words could ever express. Concluding my presentation, attendees mistakenly assumed, and then requested, my published story. The Mule is in response to both situations.

Every decade, phenomenal material keeps on coming. Some events from years gone by still cause me to belly-laugh, often at inappropriate times. Life's enjoyments and blessings are numerous. On the flip side, the Holy Spirit has carried me through grievous valleys of loss, illness, disability, marital strife, condemnation, and years of caring for my gravely ill child. Through it all, the ups and the downs, I've learned to press into Jesus through the reading of Scripture, remaining prayerful, blasting worship music (intermittent with Carole King, James Taylor, and any and all Motown), while relying on the wisdom and prayers of my family and friends. And there's the blessing: Weeping may come for a night, but rejoicing comes in the morning. Psalm 30:5

As long as I have the capacity of recall, I will continue to communicate to the glory of God, from whom all blessings flow.

In His Name,

Karen Rhea.
www.karenrhea.com

Prologue

Traversing the Usila River in a flat-bottom boat, followed by arduous hikes through the mountains, with occasional reprieve on mule-back, were all modes of transportation during my husband's medical mission trip throughout Oaxaca, Mexico. When he invited me to join him the following year, I contemplated, "Why not ride a mule? They're sure-footed and don't spook easily. If they begin to freak out, they simply stop and refuse to move forward."

The experience would likely be an improvement over my stumbling, beloved quarter horse at home in Maryland. Once every five minutes, she'd trip. Upon my command, "Step up!" Crowlena's head would elevate and for a good thirty seconds, her front legs resembled the high stepping gait of the Lipizzaner stallion. Also, my high maintenance equine loved water. Despite my futile attempts to restrain her, eyeballing a puddle, stream, or lake, her ears flashed forward and she'd trot straight into anything wet. Using her front hooves, she'd create a continuous fountain to cool off her underbelly while soaking my jeans right through to my legs. In comparison, I had to wonder, *Why not ride a low-maintenance, sturdy pack mule?*

Continuing to reassure myself, I envisioned an animal behaviorist slapping one hundred mules' hind quarters to begin navigating the treacherous switchbacks up the Grand Canyon.

My imagination went south. Planting their hooves precariously close to the edge of a path, observers likely grimaced when only ninety-nine mules made it to the top. Regardless of the one fatality, "sure-footedness" statistically became associated with the beasts of burden.

The mule I road in the jungles of Mexico was likely related to the one written off as the observational consequence in my imaginary Grand Canyon study.

Here's my true story.

Me, clueless.

Chapter 1

Arm-twisting

Matthew 5:16–*In the same way, let your light shine before others, so that they may see your good works and give glory to your Father who is in heaven.*

For decades, my husband Jim provided dental care around the globe. After his first trip to Mexico, on the way home from the airport, he appeared lost in thought and had difficulty describing the details of his trip. Fumbling through his back pack, he asked me to pull into the post office. During his flight, he packed up a dozen rolls of film to send to Seattle Film Works, a mail order film processing company. Prior to instantaneous, digital photographs, he captured images with his Canon A-1 camera.

Entering our house, he slung his duffle bag on the laundry room floor, peeled off his clothes and took a twenty minute shower. When the water turned off, he cracked the door and asked me to pour him a glass of cold milk. Apparently that had been his craving the final days of his trip. A few minutes later, I fulfilled his request, handed him the glass and he gulped it down, making an exaggerated eye roll as if he was a shark devouring its prey. Handing me back the empty glass, he walked into the bedroom, flopped down on the bed and slept for twelve hours.

The next morning, he returned to work to treat his patients. Following Cathy's appointment, she stood up and said, "It's so good to have you back, Dr. Jim. I didn't want to go to anyone else with my broken tooth."

He told her that it was typical in the mission field for patients to express their appreciation with a warm embrace. She immediately wrapped her arms around him, exclaiming, "Finally, I have permission to hug you!"

Her warmth was the best medicine a patient could give her doctor.

Jim battled fatigued for weeks, often relating the poverty of those he served in comparison to the abundance we enjoyed. Yet his demeanor lightened two weeks later when his treasure trove of memories arrived. With dozens of photographs jogging his recollections, he began sharing his adventures. Jim was bitten by the proverbial "mission bug" and I now sensed his longing to return.

Jim and his companions travel to villages to administer much-needed dental treatment.

Locals graciously shared their living quarters.

Villagers model their wares.

Children world-wide enjoy ring-around-the-rosy.

Carrying water was part of women's daily labor.

Sunday worship service.

Initially, providing rudimentary dental care in rural settings with no electricity or running water seemed nearly impossible, in comparison to the modern conveniences and high-tech
equipment my husband became accustomed to in private practice. Due to the numerous challenges he encountered, my
always-prepared, always-organized husband often mentioned
how much he needed an assistant on future trips.

Even so, his preparations proved adequate. Our living room
morphed into his packing area. I had a list I checked off as he
filled his duffle bag.

"OK, Karen, here we go. One camping headlight, extra batteries, topical numbing gel, anesthesia, four packages of long needles and four packages of short needles, four syringes, four forceps, four elevators [for rocking teeth loose], gauze, surgical gloves, and masks."

He had four plastic containers, which he filled daily with Cidex, a high-level disinfectant liquid where instruments soaked for twenty minutes following patient contact. Additional containers were filled with water to rinse off the disinfectant. Pack mules carried all supplies, including huge containers of water and a large bucket, where the patient could spit following injections and extractions. Clothing, care packages, Bibles, and the missionary's movie projector and battery pack provided education, entertainment, and gifts for anyone in need.

The learning curve on that first trip south of the border made Jim realize playing the role of the doctor, assistant, and receptionist was far from efficient. An extra set of hands providing patient care, crowd control, and clean up would have given him additional time treating patients.

Setting up his outdoor work space took about an hour. A raised platform for instruments and sterilization liquids were essential for a day's work. Left too low to the ground, village dogs would lap up anything wet, contaminating the area. Curious little kids constantly handled the shiny instruments.

The language barrier proved difficult; only men who worked closer to the city of Tuxtepec spoke some Spanish. Chinantec dialect is the primary language in remote areas of Oaxaca. Jim's interpreter couldn't communicate with villagers, so smiling, pointing, and grunting had to suffice.

Patients needed a place to sit while being treated. After bending over thirty patients in one day, Jim's crippling lower back pain set in. Only a contortionist could work on top teeth in those conditions, so villagers elevated a rickety chair on cinder bricks. It worked fairly well, raising the patient to a workable height. Yet the absence of a head rest required another set of hands to support the crown of the patient's head. The term "pulling teeth" is really the opposite of the pressure imposed on the patient. An oral surgeon's dominate arm typically resembles Popeye's, for it takes incredible strength to rock and push the root of a tooth loose before ultimately sliding it from its socket.

Even though locals were quick to assist by stabilizing the back of their friend's heads, curiosity reigned as they often stuck their heads in Jim's field of sight, simply fascinated at the instruments and precise procedure to extract teeth. His technique was so different from their own: a rock and a two by four to knock out an infected tooth, often leaving the root to fester.

Typically, Jim lined up four patients, evaluating their most pressing tooth ache with the aid of each patient pointing and grimacing. Continually adjusting his headlight, the blazing sun helped illuminate the tooth in question. This was his only diagnostic tool, as radiographs were unheard of. After pinpointing the sore molar, cuspid, bi-cuspid, or incisor, he would inject anesthesia, throw away the needle, and put that syringe into the sterilization bucket. He'd move on to inject the second patient, the third, and then the fourth in like manner.

It usually took about twenty minutes for the tooth to become totally numb before treatment began. Equal time was needed for proper sterilization of the syringe before being used on the next group of patients. Transitioning into the role of a dental assistant, he moved the clean instruments from the Cidex and rinsed them in water. Sterile needles and anesthesia were put in clean syringes for the next four patients.

Dentistry was provided during daylight, even as temperatures rose into the triple digits.

As he turned back to perform actual dentistry, it was troubling to find three out of four patients missing. He knew they were likely numb, ready for a painless extraction. It took one day to realize villagers mistakenly thought the anesthesia was the remedy for their pain. Returning to their villages, several marched back to the make-shift clinic less than satisfied, believing the doctor's medicine didn't work.

That night, after falling into a deep, exhaustive sleep, he abruptly awoke to find a woman yelling at him while pointing at one of her teeth. His interpreter dragged her out of the block-house. Jim just couldn't face the logistical issues alone on future mission trips.

Hence, next time, he wanted me to accompany him. After setting up for a day's work, he would triage patients' most pressing need. To adequately chart our progress, I would write the tooth number needing treatment on a post-it and slap it to their clothing. Learning the word for "wait" or "don't move" would help. Believing a smile would go a long way, my determined husband repeatedly brought up how much I'd love serving with him. Reminding me that I assisted him prior to managing the office, he felt my multiple skills would be useful.

Sitting on our front porch swing on a warm July evening, I had to be honest with Jim.

"I can't fathom controlling the situation. Are you serious? So, once you get your patients numb after months of misery, it sounds like I'll be herding cats. Should I wear an orange patrol belt while blowing a whistle to keep order?"

We both laughed at the absurdity of it all.

Mission work was very gratifying to Jim, and he definitely had a skill to share. Loving the outdoors, he felt it was the most exhilarating experience to bathe in a river. I pictured Water moccasins beneath me. Sleeping under the stars, he knew all the planets. He marveled at God's creation. I awaited bat attacks. The rough travel, with downright miserable conditions and uncertainty about local foods and polluted water, banished mission work from my radar. There were so many things I'd rather do.

Locals bathe and wash clothes in the Usila River, with a balsa raft in the foreground.

Six months later, the living room was once again converted into his packing area. This time, he added a gross of toothbrushes, toothpaste, and an assortment of stickers for the kids.

I noticed he was somewhat perplexed, rummaging through photos. Jim handed me a snapshot of a dozen children.

"Did you ever see this one? Check out their expressions."

Reminiscent of American Gothic photos, Indians did not smile for the camera. Yet, kids are kids and several smiled anyway. One little girl in the group couldn't contain her excitement, trying unsuccessfully to hide her giggles with a hand. A toddler wore an unbuttoned, collared shirt, displaying his belly and no underpants. Another little guy with dirty knees sported a pair of black cowboy boots. That one photo captured my heart.

Children posing for the camera.

With that sweet image planted in my mind, it took little coaxing for me to believe God was nudging me out of my comfort zone. It was time to get my passport and join my husband on his return excursion to serve the Chinantec Indians.

Chapter 2

The Adventure Begins

Romans 12:2–Do not conform yourselves to the standards of this world, but let God transform you inwardly by a complete change of your mind. Then you will be able to know the will of God—what is good and is pleasing to him and is perfect.

Our seven-year-old son Billy, or just "B" as we often called him, wanted to go too. My parents were not happy with our decision to take him, as they were totally willing to have ten days with their grandson. Yet we were resolute as our departure date, February 1992, neared. Mom and Dad drove us to Dulles International Airport. They were rarely emotional, but as we said goodbye at the boarding gate, they both fought back tears.

Our goodbyes to my parents at airport security.

As if I were Jim's priest, he couldn't hold back his confession when the 727 lifted off the runway. "Karen, I need to tell you that I strategically held back that one photograph of the kids, knowing it would convince you to come with me."

Laughing, I absolved him immediately.

Our first of three flights took us to Dallas/Ft. Worth. Billy sat in between us, enjoying his eggs, sausage, fruit, toast, and orange juice. After an hour of playing gin rummy, he put the deck back into his backpack and pulled out his Nintendo Game Boy. The final hour of the flight, he began reading his seventh book in the Boxcar Children series, which he had discovered the previous year. Packing two more books for the trip, just like his dad, he could read for hours.

On our next leg to Mexico City, Jim began to prepare B for the culture shock awaiting us. He reminded him that he would need to share his packages of peanut butter crackers when eating them in front of others. Bill interrupted his dad when he began to warn him about hazards of dirty water.

"I know, Dad. You told me to keep my eyes and mouth closed in the shower and to only brush my teeth with iodine water from the canteen."

Apparently our son had been listening.

Arriving in Mexico City, the aircraft dropped suddenly, descending into a bowl of fog.

"How does the pilot see the runway?" Billy asked.

"He's used to it. That's air pollution, not the weather," Jim responded.

When the wheels touched down, we breathed a collective sigh of relief. In the airport, the customs lines seemed endless. Our final flight was leaving within the hour and the gate was in a different terminal. Once Jim had all three of our passports back in hand, we took off running and fortunately made our connection. Settling into our seats on the short flight to Tuxtepec, we immediately dozed off, exhausted from the long day's travel.

Arriving in Veracruz.

Landing in Veracruz, we were greeted by Bob, the resident missionary. Piling our gear into his dilapidated station wagon, he yelled,

"Hold on!"

Driving like a maniac, he had obviously lived with the locals for years, fitting in fairly well. It was a two hour, hair-raising ride to Usila. Passing vehicles on the dirt shoulder of the road was common practice. Right after swerving to miss a woman walking on the shoulder of the road with a bucket of water on her head, he announced that multiple pedestrian and bicycle fatalities occurred annually. Sitting in the back seat, I threw my arm across B's chest and slammed my foot on the non-existent floorboard brake with every acceleration.

Finally, we arrived at the boarding school for at-risk young girls rescued from abuse and prostitution. I shot Jim a nasty glance for never mentioning the crazy driving we'd endure. Sheepishly, he looked away. My irritation waned when Bob's wife Flo met us with open arms.

Two young women, Ruth and Louise, joined our team. Ruth, a dental technician from Canada, and Louise, a dental assistant from the Netherlands, were welcomed additions. They were as green as I was to mission work.

I manage a smile on the rooftop of the girls' boarding house, now that the car ride is over.

Everyone fell asleep early. The heat, coupled with the humidity, was oppressive. Ten years earlier, our home in Maryland was void of air conditioning. After having it installed, we typically ran it when temperatures climbed into the eighties. There was no such luxury at our accommodations. Instead, a tiny, oscillating fan squeaked out a slight breeze.

We awoke to young girls singing in a small courtyard, as they went about their morning chores. After a hearty breakfast, Bob and Jim tossed our gear back into the station wagon and Flo drove us to the river. Our journey to the first village would take two days. Bob arranged for locals to resupply our food and water when we transferred from our three-hour boat ride to mule back.

Tooling down the Usila River into the jungles near the Guatemalan border.

Front: Me, Jim, and Billy

Background; Ruth and Louise and our guides.

During a grueling journey by pontoon boat in blistering heat, Billy dug into his backpack, pulling out his peanut butter crackers. After struggling to open the package, he pulled out one cracker as the missionary announced over the roar of the motor,

"Thanks, young man. We're all a little hungry."

Taking the package away, it was passed from person to person. Within thirty seconds, our son looked incredibly disappointed when he was handed an empty package. Everyone expressed thanks, as B got his first lesson in sharing to the point of sacrifice.

When our interminable boat ride came to an end, we all clumsily waded through shallow water and helped bring our supplies on shore. Six extra mules and several men on their own donkeys awaited our arrival. Two of the mules were loaded with our backpacks and all our possessions. The remaining four mules were for riding. Billy announced,

"Let's call this The Mule Intersection."

Billy saddled up, as we adapted from the boat to burros.

I thought for sure Billy would be placed in front of Jim on the saddle. Instead, someone hoisted him in front of one of the Indian guides and trotted out of sight. This arrangement just seemed wrong. I wondered who was riding off with my little boy. Praying for Billy's protection helped me repress my over-active imagination of impending doom. God calmed my angst by giving me a delightful traveling companion. Louise and I traveled side by side, following a guide. For hours, I had no clue as to Jim, Billy, or Ruth's location. Reassuring myself, certainly Jim was traveling with our son.

Late in the day, our guides began pointing and yelling with excitement. Villagers ran toward us from their huts as the obvious welcome wagon. How strange to see Billy running toward me with the villagers. He yelled,

"Mom, where have you been? Do you know where Dad is?"

Apparently Billy's guide made good time, prodding his donkey into a cantor with a switch for much of the trip. Another hour passed before Jim and Ruth walked into the village. What a relief to see him! We learned that much earlier in the afternoon, Ruth's mule encountered quicksand. Guides used Jim's mule to pull her mule free. After that holdup, locals insisted they walk the remainder of the day, possibly worried about their livestock.

Once all together, Bob told us that women and children would all sleep in one hut, and he and Jim would sleep outside. These accommodations, in addition to being separated all afternoon from my family, added to my growing anxiety.

A cow bell rang, indicating dinner would be served. Crowding into a smoke-filled hut, a local family served us a hearty meal. It was hard to identify much but the chicken. It was obvious they were going without in order to give us what little they had. Their children, including their daughter with Down syndrome, waited on us. They bowed their heads and prayed before we ate. Billy said it was the longest prayer he'd ever heard.

Bob responded, "Oh, Billy, they were thanking Jesus for your dad and your whole family; for Ruth and Louise and your willingness to come all the way to Oaxaca to take care of their dental needs. Then they thanked Jesus for the chicken that was big enough to share."

Meager food supplies were shared, displaying an abundance of hospitality.

During the meal, our itinerary was discussed. We would return to this village in five days and Jim would provide dental care for this group of people at the conclusion of our trip. The following morning, we faced another full day of travel through the mountains to reach the village of Santiago.

After dinner, we were instructed to be in our huts before nightfall, due to large cats that sometimes prowled into the village after dark. I could not believe Bob and Jim were sleeping outdoors! Needless to say, I was grateful for daybreak after a sleepless night.

While enjoying a generous breakfast of Spanish scrambled eggs, I remembered to take my last antibiotic for a lingering case of asthmatic bronchitis. Billy and I brushed our teeth and packed up, meeting everyone at the shoreline of the Usila River. Supplies towered atop the mules' backs. On this leg of the trip, there were only two mules available to ride. I strongly suggested Jim keep watch over B and ride together with one of the guides. A bit saddle sore from the previous day, I preferred to walk with Louise, Ruth, Bob, and the second guide.

Mistakenly, I assumed we'd all travel together until my family disappeared, rounding a bend by the river. Our guide turned the opposite direction as Bob yelled,

"See you in a few hours, guys."

Our group began climbing paths up into the mountainside. Louise and I passed the hours by getting to know one another, laughing, and even singing.

"Then sings my soul, my Savior God to thee. How great thou art. How great thou art."

Ruth often stopped, obviously exhausted, stating,

"Not another hill to climb."

Hours into our hike, my bronchitis began to flare due to the elevation. I didn't feel ill, just horribly winded. Bob felt we would meet up with Jim and Billy by lunch time. Then we'd all take a break, and I could ride.

Another four hours found us all together again, this time deep into the jungle near the Guatemalan border. It was hard to fathom how far we had come. The remoteness of the location was evident.

"Mom, Dad's mule is nuts. He chased a bull and Dad could hardly control him!"

Following a quick bite to eat and warm bottles of Coke, Jim realized I was wheezing and insisted I ride his mule. Bob mounted Billy's mule. Father and son would hike for the remainder of the day.

Little did I know, our real adventure was about to begin.

Hiking through the jungles.

Jim prepares to dismount, giving me his mule.

As I saddled up, Jim and B picked up their pace, walking ahead of me. My mule began to stumble his way up the steep incline, so my guide grabbed the reins from my hands. He stepped in front of me and began walking backwards, attempting to muscle the mule by pulling the reins as he ascended up the slippery, uneven grade. The mule protested with a snort, and rocks started to give way under his hooves. My saddle slid back toward his hindquarters. I yelled,

"Jim, this doesn't feel safe!"

He spun around, smiled, and called out,

"Just hold on!"

That's exactly what I was doing. Surely this mule was more surefooted than my clumsy quarter horse back home. Certainly he would regain his footing. But with no reins, a slipping saddle, and the trail collapsing beneath us, I had no control. Neither did my guide. His eyes bulged, as his own boots begin to slide. My steed's front legs buckled and the reins snapped from the guide's grip. We were going down!

Chapter 3

The Rescue

Matthew 25:35-40- *For I was hungry and you gave me food, I was thirsty and you gave me drink, I was a stranger and you welcomed me, I was naked and you clothed me, I was sick and you visited me, I was in prison and you came to me. Then the righteous will answer him, saying, "Lord, when did we see you hungry and feed you, or thirsty and give you drink? And when did we see you a stranger and welcome you, or naked and clothe you? And when did we see you sick or in prison and visit you?" And the King will answer them, "Truly, I say to you, as you did it to one of the least of these my brothers, you did it to me."*

After hearing a strange rustling through the thick jungle foliage, Jim looked back. I was gone and so was the mule. Half the group retreated down the steep, rocky incline, while remaining team members peered over a cliff, yelling,
"She's down! Karen's down!"

23

Joining stunned onlookers to see what all the commotion was about, he peered far over the bluff in disbelief. There I lay face up, bloody, and eerily still, like a sacrificial offering upon a bolder. Horrified, Jim took off in a sprint to reach me with Billy on his heels. He was in a nightmare where every attempt to move forward puts the destination further away.

Reaching the jungle floor, he steamrolled his way through several onlookers gathering around my body. Jim knelt, gently lifting my head onto his lap as sticky liquid poured into his hands, saturating his T-shirt. My head bled profusely. At that moment, my body shifted; only then did he realize I was alive. With a blank stare, I began whispering my three questions and one statement,

"Is the mule ok? What did I do wrong? I think my back is broken. Can we go home now?"

And so my rote statements continued for hours. Speculations as to what happened murmured in local dialect and English. Bob pointed high up the precipice and announced,

"Karen likely separated from the mule mid-air, striking her head on that jagged rock before landing on this bolder. She must have fallen at least twenty-five feet."

In and out of consciousness, not only was I in shock, momentarily Jim was too. Glancing up at our little boy, he focused on Billy's distraught, blue, watery eyes under the brim of his baseball cap. Putting a hand to his own cheek, my husband became aware of his own tears. Our family's grave plight flooded Jim's mind, as his fear morphed into determination to get me the medical help I so desperately needed.

Our group's morning trek had taken hours. Devising the only plan available, Bob sent our Indian guide back to his village to seek additional help. Sprinting out of sight, everyone knelt, laying the palms of their hands on Jim, Billy, and me. The missionary boldly cried,

"Father, God, be with our sister, Karen. We know this situation grieves you as it does us. We beg you for added protection, aid, and healing. Give Jim and Billy comfort. Help us rely on your life sustaining, saving grace. Enable us all to do your bidding. Guide us, we pray. Amen."

Two of the women and several other locals accompanying our medical team prepared to make the journey back to the village. Acutely aware of my dire situation, Jim had to insist our reluctant, little guy go with the team. B's hands were tucked deep in his pockets and his only protest was repeatedly shaking his head no.

"Buddy, you have to go now. I'll take care of your mom, but when the Indians get here, they'll move so fast and we'll have trouble keeping up. You have to go. I'm so sorry, Billy."

Jim couldn't tell Billy, but our predicament could actually worsen. Jaguars roamed the mountains at nightfall. Guilt flooded Jim's soul, as he grieved our decision to not leave our little boy in the safe arms of his grandparents. Looking up from my blank stare, he watched B march off with the others in his new, red hiking boots bought specifically for this adventure. His baseball cap was now turned backwards on his head. He always wore it accordingly on serious hikes.

There was nothing left to say. Bob and Jim's silence was drowned out by noises echoing through the jungle. Screeching parrots occasionally covered my whispered pleas to return home. Holding me, helplessness increased with every passing hour. Jim did the only thing he knew to do. He fed me narcotics intended for his patients, following difficult tooth extractions. Then, out of total desperation to prevent infection, if I was able to survive transport to a hospital, he finely crushed antibiotic tablets into water from his canteen. Exposing the gapping gash through my thick brown hair, he poured the concoction into the deep wound.

Getting me back to the village would be no small feat.

Bob told Jim that he believed they would be able to get me back to the small village from which we had started. His bigger concern was the challenge of getting me back to the city of Tuxtepec, where medical care might be available. It was Sunday and small airplanes simply never flew in the jungles on Sundays. There were no phones and simply no way to communicate with anyone. Jim silently prayed, heavy with grief interrupted only by squealing howler monkeys, squawking birds, and a visiting iguana doing a dance on my chest. For a second, he thought he was hallucinating until Bob swatted the reptile away.

"Is the mule ok? What did I do wrong? I think my back is broken. Can we go home now?"

Temperatures rose into triple digits. Just when the canopy of the jungle failed to dim the rays of the sun, voices and footsteps approached. Finally, a small group of rescuers from the village arrived and began devising their plan. Jim's glimmer of hope faded when they tried to strap my wrists and ankles by rope to a pole, as if I were a dead animal. Intervening by untying the ropes, Jim's disapproval was interpreted by Bob. Understanding, they began chopping branches and pulling down vines from the trees, constructing a balsa wood-and-vine stretcher. Laying out a bed roll, they lifted me onto the make-shift transport.

Paths were non-existent for much of the trek.

Villagers carried me over the mountains, taking the shortest route but not necessarily the easiest path. With skillful deliberation, a path was created by two men swinging their machetes. A woman continually shaded me with an umbrella. Throughout the day, the vines would bow on my stretcher, causing me to sink, which increased the pressure on my back, and thus increased my pain. Setting me on the ground to tighten the support, prayerful foreign petitions to Jesus filled the air. My agony subsided, interrupted with the sensation of hands covering me head to toe. Utterances of unfamiliar words pierced through my pain, and the sweetest calm and an internal assurance that all would be "ok" washed over me.

Jim's eyes flashed toward Bob's. In unison, they stated the obvious,

"Look at her face."

Following hours of groaning and repetitive pleas, my brow ceased to furrow in pain and an expression of contentment appeared.

After a communal water consumption, the stretcher was lifted once again. Hoisting me up for the continued journey, I gasped in agony as rescuers forged through the jungle in double step speed.

"Is the mule ok? What did I do wrong? I think my back is broken. Can we go home now?"

The brutal terrain didn't dissuade my rescuers' goal.

The previous day, Jim's seven-hour hike produced deep blisters on his feet. Now he could barely walk without excruciating pain shooting through his heels and toes. Hours into the trek, Jim lost sight of the rescue party. Voices disappeared, and he found himself alone. Standing at a fork in the jungle, in utter desperation, he began to weep into the palms of his hands.

Behind him, he suddenly heard a horse whinny, and hooves slapping the dirt path. Jim looked up. An old man dismounted and attempted to hand him the reins. Blinking away tears, Jim didn't quite know what to do. The old guy took Jim's wrist, put the reins in his hand, and smiled broadly, exposing missing teeth numbers seven, eight, and likely number ten, right in the front. They nodded at one another as Jim mounted.

Rearing up, the horse immediately galloped as if he'd been slapped by a crop. It must have been a good ten minutes when Jim's growing relief turned to despair. Ahead, he saw two paths. Not a clue as to where to go, he was unable to muscle the reins in a futile attempt to slow the galloping horse. Instead, his steed went into fifth gear, breaking into a run while veering left. Five minutes later, he slowed to a trot. The river rushed below and Jim was able to see my stretcher being taken across to the bank on the other side. He led the horse down switchbacks to the shallowest point of entry into the water.

Aware we were in a river, I could feel the rushing current below. Turning my head left, then right, I saw the straining of men's wrists holding my stretcher. Glancing up, I saw the sweet eyes of a dark-skinned woman holding a black umbrella over my head. The sun was so intense, my jeans were soaked from sweat. In my mind, I questioned why they didn't simply lower me into the water to cool me off.

Jim watched my rescue team navigate white water rapids in the Usila River. Holding me high above the rushing river, men strained to keep their balance in the fast current.

Dismounting the horse, Jim was momentarily perplexed. Standing beside him was the old man with a toothless, warm grin. As before, Jim noticed his specific missing teeth. Handing him the reins, they nodded at one another as Jim waded deep into the river. His mind immediately shifted back to me and Billy, wondering how this day would end.

Chapter 4

Child-like Faith

Matthew 19:14—*Jesus said, "Let the little children come to me, and do not hinder them, for the kingdom of heaven belongs to such as these."*

B ack in the village, our little boy sat all afternoon on the dirt airstrip in the sweltering heat. Team members brought him bottled water, while encouraging him to join them in a hut to escape the sun. Billy opened his Teenage Mutant Ninja Turtles fanny pack, took out a package of peanut butter crackers, and munched away while stating,

"No thank you. I need to stay here and pray for Jesus to send an airplane so we can bring my mom home."

One by one, team members and a handful of Christian villagers would join him and pray for an airplane to arrive.

An airplane arrives on a Sunday.

Everyone heard it. The hum of an old Cessna resounded above the clearing, where our tenderhearted, little boy bowed his head all afternoon. Villagers ran to the dirt airstrip, madly waving for the pilot to land. Shortly after the wheels touched down, kicking up clouds of dust and debris, our son ran up to the pilot. In perfect Spanish, he pleaded,

"Por favor espera. Mi mama puede haber muerto y mi papa la esta trayendo aqui."

One of the dental technicians was shocked at his ability to communicate so effectively. He told her about the Spanish emersion program he began in kindergarten.

"If my teacher, Senora Faz, was here, she might correct what I just tried to say."

When the English-speaking team asked him what he said, their hearts sunk with his translation. I think I said,

"Please wait. My mom may have died and my dad is bringing her here."

33

The pilot and his friend agreed to wait for a period of time.

Shaded under the wing of the airplane, Louise comforts Billy as they await our return.

Jim, along with the servants who sacrificially carried me for hours, were stunned to see the aircraft. Billy ran toward his dad while pointing at the airplane.

"Look Dad, Jesus said, 'Yes.'"

Villagers gather around me after I was transferred to a cot. The woman with the closed, black umbrella shaded me the entire trek. Billy stands back, hesitating to approach.

Jim recognized the pilot from the previous year; he was identified as the local drug runner by villagers. When the pilot extended his hand, with gratitude, Jim mistakenly grasped his palm firmly and shook it. Pulling away, the pilot glared at the gringo and again extended his hand, palm up. Now Jim understood and gave him all the money he had in his pocket.

"That's all I have." When Billy translated, the pilot snapped back at Billy. His dad asked what he said; Billy's reply was comical.

"He said I sound Cuban and he needs more money when we land in Tuxtepec."

Sure enough, B's teacher, Senora Faz, was Cuban.

The pilot and his accomplice began pulling the two seats out of the back of their flying mule. Several huge boxes were left inside the cabin. Jim sat on one and Billy on another.

My stretcher laid between them. Instructions were barked in Spanish to not open the boxes.

Accommodations are made for our family on the airplane.

A full moon appeared as the engines revved up. Superstitious villagers clamored for a closer look at our son. In awe, they peered into the cargo area, believing he had magic powers due to the airplane's arrival; if they only understood. One little boy, their neighbors who called Jesus their Savior, and all who prayed that day had the only power needed. God answered in the affirmative to our advocate, the Holy Spirit.

John 14:26 - *But the Helper, the Holy Spirit, whom the Father will send in my name, he will teach you all things and bring to your remembrance all that I have said to you.*

Children ran behind the airplane, enjoying the wind the propellers created after a still, hot day.

Thirty minutes into our flight, my retching and tears were now constant. In and out of shock, the bumpy ride kept me pleading,

"Please tell him to take off. The runway is too rough. I can't take this anymore."

Billy no longer needed to be brave. Now in his dad's presence, tears welled in his eyes and he broke down, as exhaustion and the reality of our predicament required reassurance.

"Dad, are you sure this airplane is safe? Look at that duct tape wrapped all around the wing. And there's more there, and there, and also there! Remember when we were following Uncle Tom's truck to his house and his back fender flew off, and we almost ran over it? You thought it was funny and said how everyone thinks you can count on duct tape to fix anything. This won't be funny if the wing falls off."

Now they were reassuring one another.

Jim unsuccessfully tried to push away suspicions of a spinal cord injury. Thoughts of a debilitating brain injury crashed in on him. Tears flowed freely as he prayed. During that moment of speculation and the horror of what could be, Jim thought back to the old, toothless man. How could it have been humanly possible for him to arrive at the river at the exact moment he jumped off the horse? And how did the horse know the way? How odd to recall his missing tooth numbers upon his arrival and his final destination. Only a dentist would have noticed. An angel?

Hebrews 1:14 - *Are they not all ministering spirits sent forth to minister for those who will inherit salvation?*

Chapter 5

Fear and Fortitude

Isaiah 41:10–Fear not, for I am with you; be not dismayed, for I am your God; I will strengthen you, I will help you, I will uphold you with my righteous right hand.

After landing at the Usila airstrip, the pilot disappeared, leaving his buddy to eyeball Jim with mounting suspicion. The pit in my husband's stomach grew as time passed. Certainly the pilot was seeking help and not abandoning us. An hour later, Jim recognized Bob's station wagon approaching. His wife Flo returned with the pilot. After embracing Billy and Jim, she handed the pilot more cash. Now satisfied with their payment, a few parting words gave the cagy duo reason to return to their cockpit.

Settling into Bob and Flo's car, B sat in the front passenger seat next to Flo. Jim took up his previous position of holding my head in his lap. My body stretched across the back seat, as we steeled ourselves for a ride to a local clinic. Billy looked at his TMNT watch.

"Dad, Mom fell at lunch time; that was over twelve hours ago. I'm sort of hungry and sick of peanut butter crackers."

I was in and out of consciousness. Jim kept insisting I drink the iodine-tasting water from his canteen. His eyes continually welled with tears.

"I'm so sorry, Karen. Yes, I know the water tastes bad, but remember, it tastes safe. I promise I'll get us home. I love you."

Arriving after midnight, we found the clinic closed and were forced to remain in Flo's car until Dr. Garcia arrived. In the wee hours of the morning, he unlocked his facility.

He and Jim put me on a gurney and wheeled me inside. I was now positioned underneath a dim light attached to a ceiling fan. After fumbling through a few drawers, Dr. Garcia located thick cord resembling macramé rope which he used to suture the back of my head. No anesthesia was available. It was the first time I experienced pain in my open wound. X-rays would need to be taken the following day.

Becoming acutely aware of my surroundings, the pain in my back became unbearable. Billy sat on a stool by my side. In pure exhaustion, both of his arms wrapped around my neck; his head tucked into my side. He had fallen asleep. Looking up, my thoughts focused on the fact I survived something horrible, yet I worried that this wobbly fan spinning over my head was bound to detach and kill me.

I lost all composure when I thought of my parents. "Whatever you do, don't tell Mom and Dad about this. Promise me, Jim!"

The same thought entered his mind. He assured me they weren't expecting our return for another week, and we would keep this to ourselves for as long as possible. My parents had buried my only sister nine years earlier. I couldn't bear the thought of how helpless they would feel if they learned of my accident. How could they handle any more grief? Did they want Billy to stay with them during our trip because they had a premonition about the risks of him joining us? Maybe they simply possessed more common sense than me.

Jim and Dr. Garcia moved me to a bed with the aid of a young woman. Getting on my side in a Cleopatra pose brought momentary relief. Yet ghastly pain returned within seconds, and I realized there was no reprieve in sight. Jim pulled up a chair next to my bed and leaned into the mattress by my legs. Billy sat on his lap. Throughout the coming hours, the narcotics were no more effective than aspirin. Roosters began crowing before daybreak in a deafening chorus.

It was time for Dr. Garcia to determine a diagnosis. I was loaded back into the station wagon for a ride across the city. Arriving, Flo interpreted as I was brought into a less than sterile room with a wooden table. An antiquated, large machine was wheeled by my side. Jim stood to my right and an attendant to my left, supporting me under my arms as I slowly stood up. Everyone was talking at once. Suddenly, Flo yelled, "Now!" The attendant slammed my shoulders onto a table, bending me at the waist. When the button for the x-ray machine was pressed, there was a loud buzzing noise. I screamed in agony, drowning out all noises in the room. When my knees buckled and I fell to the floor, I heard Jim yell in anger.

Despite a population of approximately 140,000 in Tuxtepec, no one knew how to take an x-ray. After loading me back into the station wagon, Flo cracked the windows for air and drove slowly to the clinic in silence. Following that clinical disaster, a neurosurgeon from Veracruz was contacted and planned on arriving the following afternoon.

The following day, when the surgeon arrived, Flo encouraged Billy to interpret conversations between Dr. Garcia and his associate.

"Dad, the new doctor thinks Mom needs medicine because her brain might swell. Also, he's talking about her back."

The neurosurgeon was concerned that I was totally unaware of my head trauma. Displaying intermittent confusion was added cause for concern. Intravenous steroids were administered to arrest possible swelling in my brain. The doctor's strong suspicion of spinal cord damage could neither be confirmed nor dismissed. The severity of my injuries were a mystery. Black and blue bruising covered me from my upper thighs to my waist. How odd to experience numbness, not unlike my epidural before childbirth. But the throbbing never stopped. Unable to lift my feet off the ground and totally dependent on the female helpers for all my needs, I just wanted to go home.

Closing my eyes, I prayed for an escape. Deep rapid eye movement deprivation, due to excruciating pain, made it impossible to dream away my living nightmare. Mid-morning, the smell of raw chicken wafted through the steel bars above my bed. Most of the window panes were broken. Rows of grills, filled with charcoal, doused in lighter fluid lined the sidewalk just outside my room. Once lit, smoke drifted inside. The odor of chicken was nauseating. A wet washcloth over my face helped. Laughter and occasional disagreements between chefs, accented by blaring car horns, stirred me from moments of rest. Nausea and severe pain were my constant companions.

For forty-eight hours, Jim and Billy wouldn't leave my side. Flo brought meals. She washed my filthy clothes and placed my folded underwear, gym shorts, and T-Shirts on a table next to my bed. Flo escorted Billy outside so Jim and Dr. Garcia's medical aid could wash me.

In order to change my clothes, Jim supported me under my arms to raise me from the bed to a standing position. Mistakenly, Jim and the aid attempted to swing my legs off the bed. It was excruciating. I did better moving my legs slowly. Sitting, bent at the waist, was a nightmare; I needed immediate help standing. Once standing, Jim gently lifted each of my feet off the floor to pull off my jeans and underwear and slide on clean clothes.

Another big mistake was assuming a bed pan would be helpful. Lifting my hips caused me to scream and faint. So the only alternative was to figure out a way to move twenty feet toward a toilet. Again, I needed help to stand. They tried to have me sit on a desk chair with wheels, but it was too painful. So out of desperation, I figured out how to inch myself across the floor by scooting my feet together, heel toe, heel toe. It took a long time, so I needed to do this frequently to avoid urinating in the bed. Maneuvering myself from point A to point B felt like a huge breakthrough. Also, getting off the lumpy mattress and standing upright for a moment brought momentary relief.

Missing window panes in my rudimentary clinic.

Becoming aware of my family's exhaustion,
"Jim, please take Billy to the mission house to sleep at night."
He argued with me; yet Flo joined in my insistence.

"It's only fifteen minutes away. We can get you rest, showered, and back here early each morning, and the aid will be by her side all night."

Billy stands outside of the clinic.
To his left is the window into my room. The frosted areas are glass.
Clear sections are broken windows, likely never to be replaced.

Reluctantly, they left late that evening. Each night was reminiscent of the previous ones; painful and lonely. I had no idea how long I would remain at the clinic. So naturally, I loved seeing my family come through the door each morning. Jim looked weary and conflicted; attentive to me yet distracted, likely reliving my accident. Whoever's pet pig kept visiting proved a comical distraction for us all. Billy entertained himself with his Game Boy and a deck of cards. After tiring of his Teenage Mutant Ninja Turtle's game, he'd suggest,

"Hey Mom, teach me how to play clock solitaire. Do you want to try rummy? Pop taught me how to play and win."

Passing time.

Disobeying visitation hours.

That small pig visited daily. Snorting, he'd push his snout against my hand for a scratch on the neck. Porky Pig's presence reminded me of my family dog snuggling by my side. Lizards mated on the walls. I was less a fan of reptiles, but counting geckos passed the hours.

45

When I was lucid, Jim and I discussed our predicament and plan of escape.

In 1992, we had declined travel insurance. A medical air transport from Veracruz to New Orleans would have cost $10,000. I learned Jim and Billy would not be permitted to accompany me, and my protest was absolute. The three of us would somehow get home together.

Dr. Garcia, intrigued by Jim's volunteer work, asked if he could serve alongside him. Now that our team made their long journey back from the jungle, Flo stayed by my side, allowing Jim, Louise and Ruth to set up a clinic outside Tuxtepec. Dr. Garcia joined them, providing medical care at no charge to his own people. The experience proved gratifying, and he said so.

Dr. Garcia, Louis, Dr. Rhea, Ruth, and Billy. The dental chair is raised on cinder bricks.

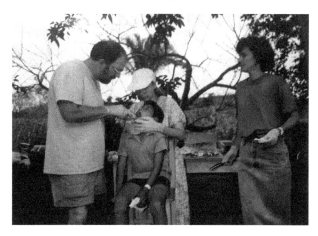

There was plenty of work to do.

Dr. Garcia provided free medical care for his impoverished people.

Billy entertains teenagers with his artwork, drawing all the
Teenage Mutant Ninja Turtles.

After five days in Dr. Garcia's clinic, I apparently became a force to be reckoned with, believing I could make the trip home via commercial airlines. Standing on my own, I wanted to prove I could manage the travel to Veracruz. I actually believed that one accomplishment was adequate proof of my endurance to manage the lengthy travel ahead.

Flo obliged and made our arrangements. Bob would drive us back to Heriberto Jara International Airport in Veracruz. I laid across the back seat and encouraged Billy to sit beside me. Jim sat in the suicide seat. Bracing myself for a wild ride was unnecessary. Unlike the unnerving trip upon our arrival, Bob carefully navigated the rough, pothole-littered highway.

Less than an hour into our trip, I needed to use a bathroom. There wasn't one, anywhere. Bob pulled over to the side of the highway. Billy hopped in the seat that his dad previously occupied. Now Bob engaged our son in conversation, as Jim assisted me out of the car and supported me by wrapping his arms just above my waist. He purposely left the back car door open as a shield. With no other options, I urinated. Quickly

48

it became apparent that nothing about our travel back to the United States would be easy. Another fifteen minutes passed, as Jim cleaned me up, pulled up my shorts, and got me back in the car. Billy stayed up front. Back in our familiar seats, with Jim by my side, I rested my head on his lap. He stroked the top of my scalp gently with his fingertips. His soothing touch helped me doze off. I stirred when I felt Jim's lips touch my ear, as he whispered,

"We're at the airport, sweetie."

Parking the station wagon in a "no parking" zone at the entrance to the airport, Bob and a police officer were engaged in a serious conversation. A wheelchair appeared. Confusion swarmed my thoughts, as too many people were attempting to help me get situated. Desperately, I looked for Jim and Billy. My little boy's voice drew my attention to the back of the car. There, Jim pulled out our duffle bags and slung them over his back.

Escorting our family through the terminal, Bob helped Jim lift me out of the wheelchair. From the runway, they painstakingly carried me up the staircase and into the entrance of the plane. When they put me down and my feet touched the floor, I had no other choice but to scoot my way to my seat assignment. Flight attendants were now becoming frustrated, as my slow movements caused by my injuries were delaying take-off. Our goodbyes were brief. The Aeromexico flight took off for Mexico City. We were heading home.

Chapter 6

Getting Home

Philippians 4:13–*I can do all things through
him who strengthens me.*

E ven though I was in and out of consciousness on that first
flight, our journey from Mexico City to Dallas and finally
Dallas to DC remains excruciatingly clear. There was no relief
from pain, even though I ingested enough narcotics to sedate
an elephant.

Wheelchairs were provided for me to go from gate to gate
in Mexico City and Dallas-Ft. Worth. But I had to be carried
up the stairs from the runway to the smiling flight attendant
welcoming me into the airplanes. Once on board, Billy led the
way and pointed out my seat. I'd scoot down the aisle by shuf-
fling heel, toe, heel, toe to my seat number, often located in the
back of the plane. Jim stayed close behind me as a buffer, pro-
tecting me from passengers shoving carry-on luggage in close
proximately to my back.

Boarding our final flight in Dallas-Ft. Worth, I was inching
my way through first class.

"Hey what happened to you? You look pretty beat up."

"Well, the mule I was riding fell off a 25 ft. cliff."

"Here's my card. Let's sue the bastards."

Uncertain as to how to respond, I accepted the attorney's business card. Jim looked like he was going to explode in fury. I tried to soothe him by stroking his hand. He snapped the card from me and flicked it into the man's lap, exclaiming,

"What do you think you'll get, moccasins and a hut? Why don't you offer my injured wife the seat you're occupying? That would be helpful."

The ambulance-chasing attorney looked down and gulped his cocktail, averting his eyes by pretending to read his Wall Street Journal. We were back in the litigious, scapegoating US of A. I continued to inch my way to seat 24B. Billy and Jim sat behind me.

During three flights, sitting for hours took on a whole new meaning of torture. I also lacked the security of my husband's hand, as we were never able to sit together. When the wheels touched the runway at Washington National Airport, Jim let me know he contacted Jimmy, his seventeen- year-old son, to meet us in baggage. Unbeknownst to me, failing to allow my parents' insight into my accident put added pressure on Jim. Had they known, they could have arranged medical transport when we finally made it home.

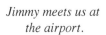

Jimmy meets us at the airport.

Now in the car, I insisted on going straight home, unable to imagine being subjected to sitting hours in an emergency room. The four steps into our house seemed incidental, when compared to the endless staircases leading up to the airplanes. Billy got his desk chair on wheels and escorted me across the tile floors in the kitchen to my bedroom. I was so incredibly weak, the ride to our bedroom, despite the pain was a relief. Our family dogs were going crazy in the backyard, wanting nothing more than a welcome home hug.

Once I was settled in my bed, Jim called our family physician. Now it was time for me to phone my parents and break the news. We were home one day earlier than planned. Mom asked, "What's happened? You weren't supposed to be home until tomorrow night."

After giving her a quick summary, she interrupted me, indicating they'd be at the house within the hour.

Everyone arrived at once. Mom and Dad stood by in horror, while Dr. Margolis looked at my back and legs covered in deep bruises. I could only stand with assistance. Unlike my previous ability to shuffle, now my feet may as well have been nailed to the floor. Crying freely, I fainted.

"I'll call an ambulance. She has to go to the hospital now. This could likely be a spinal cord injury. I'll call Suburban Hospital and she'll be admitted."

Aware of the medics in my bedroom, I begged not to go to the ER. Dr. Margolis reassured me that a room in critical care awaited my arrival. Also, Suburban was not the closest hospital to our home, but it was a trauma hospital.

Mom, who never cursed, walked out of the room, burst into tears, and yelled,

"Dammit. This is not happening."

After an uneventful, forty-five minute ride to Suburban Hospital in Bethesda, Maryland, I was admitted. Yet my blood pressure was so low, 60/36, that it was against hospital policy to administer narcotics. Jim gave me the only remaining Tylenol with codeine in his pocket and then proceeded to go ballistic on my behalf.

Prior to my CT scan, an IV was finally started and I was finally given pain meds. My orthopedist, whom I would come to know well, entered my room with the report in hand. He revealed the extent of my injuries, along with my bleak prognosis. Jim and I kept locking eyes, as we struggled to comprehend all that was being thrown at us.

"Your concussion will likely cause memory problems for an undetermined time period, requiring occupational therapy. You have a bi-lateral fractured pelvis, crushed sacrum, and, no doubt, severe nerve damage. Your right hip has dropped three-quarters of an inch. Once the physical therapist teaches you how to walk again, you will have a pronounced limp. The sacral nerve at the base of the spine affects bladder and bowel control."

All I could think was, "Lovely."

"Surgery to repair your pelvic fractures is out of the question. Your spinal cord is grossly inflamed. Actually, do not let anyone touch you with a scalpel. Any repair could cause permanent spinal injury. In fact, it's unbelievable that you are not paralyzed or dead. More people bleed to death from a pelvic fracture than any other bone fracture in the body. This is because the pelvic cavity fills with blood and the injured person bleeds to death. Your husband likely saved your life by giving you so many narcotics, slowing down the blood flow."

Chapter 7

Pain and Uncertainty

Philippians 3:8–Indeed, I count everything as loss because of the surpassing worth of knowing Christ Jesus my Lord. For his sake I have suffered the loss of all things and count them as rubbish, in order that I may gain Christ.

I was confined to bed for six months. At thirty-seven years old, I could barely comprehend the thought of being totally dependent on others for every need, while my body slowly healed. My doctor instructed me to sell my horse, telling me I would never ride again. Critical injuries sustained without proper medical care can cause a body to suffer early aging and eventually possible auto-immune complications. He told me after two years of recovery, I would know the extent of the nerve pain I would be destined to endure.

On my seventh day in the hospital, the physical therapist needed to teach me to walk up four steps to enter our house. The feeling of helplessness crashed over me with each word of instruction.

"Try lifting your left heel. That was good. Now, your toes. This time, when you lift your heel, you need to bend your knee.

At home, you'll only have one railing, so you need to let go with your right hand. I'm right behind you. Now see if you can raise that foot onto the next step."

During that one-hour session, I kept bursting into tears, sobbing uncontrollably. Even so, mission accomplished, and I was released from intensive care and brought home.

As I entered a grueling season of recovery, I questioned my decision to join Jim in Mexico. Was it for the adventure? Was it for the applause of friends? Over the next six weeks, I spiraled into depression, wondering if I had mistakenly heard God's affirmative prompting to go on that disastrous trip. My poor husband felt so guilty. My little boy hated leaving my side. Mom and Dad had buried my only sister, Sue, and now I was disabled. Their grief resurfaced. Everyone was traumatized. Surely, I had made the worst mistake of my life.

I didn't think it was possible, but the pain from my nerve damage worsened as the weeks ticked by. Without warning, fire raced up my spine to my neck. Then the back of my tongue would momentarily freeze. Just as suddenly, the red-hot coals radiated back down my spinal cord, searing my rectum and inner thigh. Gasping, my body twitched as I'd try unsuccessfully to twist my torso, in a futile attempt to stop the stinging and internal inferno. This happened several times an hour, waking me night and day.

Jim returned to his private dental practice, treating patients all day, taking care of our family each evening, and caring for my every need through the night. These demands allowed him very little sleep.

One Friday afternoon, my doctor changed me from one narcotic to another, producing wicked drug withdrawal. I thought bugs were crawling all over me, as uncontrollable diarrhea and vomiting added to the horror. Cleaning up after me, while unsuccessfully diverting my attention from hallucinations, seemed hopeless.

"Look at me. No, there's nothing there, Karen. Look at me. You know I wouldn't lie to you. Here's a cool washcloth. Let me wipe your legs. No, bugs are not on the washcloth. There are no bugs on my neck either. Trust me, babe. OK, we're going to clean you up. It will be alright."

When it dawned on him what was happening, he placed a previously discontinued narcotic on my tongue and managed to have me swallow a gulp of water. Within twenty minutes, the violent withdrawal stopped, my eyes closed, and I fell asleep.

I wondered how Jim and I would navigate our new normal. My frailty was not going away anytime soon, if ever. I watched helplessly as Jim fell into a deep depression. He became sullen and withdrawn. Even so, he stayed by my side every moment he was not at work. Unsuccessfully, I tried to encourage Jim to sleep in our guest bedroom, especially on weeknights before seeing patients.

"No way. I'm not leaving you."

Early evening, I would hear him outside my bedroom door, "Come on, B. Let's do your homework with Mom. Yes. I left the TV tray set up in front of the chair."

When daily visitors filled my bedroom, Jim exited in desperate need of privacy. Repeated enquiries from family and friends about my pain and progress exhausted him. He had no choice but to endure these same concerns from his patients throughout his work day, often causing him to become emotional and fall behind on his schedule. I could tell the repetition of my daily struggles and the constant flood of people wore down my introverted husband.

Saturdays were the easiest day to arrange actual help with household chores. My close friend thought a Sean Connery film would be a good escape for Jim. We had seen all the James Bond movies, so it made sense that seeing the actor in a different roll could be fun. When he returned home, I asked him about the show. Visibly upset, he relayed that Medicine Man took place in the Amazon rainforest and the actress traveling with Sean Connery fell off a cliff. This scene was way too reminiscent of my fall. That was his last "date" with one of my friends.

As I became more mobile, graduating from a walker to crutches, Jim broke down in humiliation.

"I'm so sorry I didn't listen to you. You knew it wasn't safe. I told you to hold on and you listened to me. I've done this to you. I'll never forgive myself, and you never should either."

Now I felt a constant need to alleviate his guilt. We had further obstacles to face.

Before we met, Jim was an avid bicycler and horseback rider. He was an excellent student and loved history and literature. Often, he read three novels at once. An introvert, he was in need of down-time to rejuvenate. Not me. Struggling in scholastics, I was social to the core. A proverbial extrovert, I was in my element surrounded by friends and family. Any adventure worthy of a good story intrigued me.

Initially, when we met, our attraction to one another was solely based on our like-minded humor, so I thought. After we married, Jim admitted falling in love with me the first time he witnessed me easily ski down a black diamond. I found hiking and climbing to the top of waterfalls in North Carolina exhilarating. Whitewater rafting was almost as much fun for me as a rollercoaster at the Montgomery County Agricultural Fair in Maryland. We both played golf, although it came easier to me than him because I learned as a kid. Jim taught me how to horseback ride. He grew up on western tack and road like a cowboy. Often, we'd saddle up our horses, Sundance and Crowlena, and barrel through the trails in our hometown of Boyds. We never tired of adventure together; in fact, it was the sweet spot in our relationship. Now what?

Severe, chronic pain can warp hope, warp truth, and warp a zeal for life.

Chapter 8

A Gift of Perspective

Hebrews 6:10–*God is not unjust; he will not forget your work and the love you have shown him as you have helped his people and continue to help them.*

To be by my side, once a week, my mom took a day of leave from her job as payroll administrator at CPSC, Consumer Product Safety Commission. Bringing the mail into the bedroom, she said,

"Karen, there's a big envelope from Mexico."

Curious, I asked her to open it. Pulling out the contents, we were stunned to see multiple photographs of my rescue. Jim and I were unaware Bob had a camera and had captured moments throughout that day. How riveting to see the images of myself being carried across the river and up through the mountains. My stoic mom could not hold back her tears. After regaining her composure, she read the letter out loud. Flo's story thwarted the discouragement that had been mounting for many months.

Bob had just recently revisited the people who rescued me. Villagers swarmed him upon arrival, asking if I had survived. They were holding on to deep grief, believing I likely died.

Though rich in faith, unfortunate circumstances and physical ailments created cruel persecution from their neighbors. The village was steeped in superstition. So, worshipping one God while enduring hardships or having bad luck befall believers was considered bad juju.

Tribal leaders prompted ridicule toward my rescuers and their families, believing their witch doctor should have been trusted rather than the outsider, Dr. Jim. They believed that betrayal likely led to my accident and death. Yet when word spread of my survival, others questioned whether the curse even existed.

Twenty-five years earlier, a doctor had come from the United States to serve in the jungles. Following engine trouble, his airplane slammed into a mountain near the very village we had stayed the night before my fall. The Indians rescued the doctor and the pilot. Their predicament resembled the seriousness of my situation. Village elders relayed the story of that rescue to their children and subsequently their grandchildren as a testimony of Jesus permitting them to serve as His hands and feet. Those who rescued me were the grandchildren of those who saved the men in the airplane crash decades earlier.

In her letter, Flo explained, "The Indians living in poverty feel humiliation when receiving help from outsiders because they are unable to repay the kindness shown. You thought you were sent to Oaxaca to help your husband treat the impoverished Indians. When in fact, God used you in a mightier way than you could have ever dreamt. Your survival is being told to the next generation."

From the moment they learned of my recovery, they were filled with total jubilation, explaining to everyone in the village that Jesus not only allowed them to rescue me but the dentist would return. Their skeptical neighbors in the village began asking questions about the God of the Bible after learning I lived.

My growing confusion and doubts as to why I joined Jim in Mexico was removed with Flo's words. Mistakenly, I thought I was going to Mexico to help Jim provide dental care. Instead, God used me to restore dignity to the Chinantec people. My perspective was adjusted. I was learning much and had much to learn.

My litany of cries and heartache lessened, as I'd simply still my thoughts and listen for His voice, His comfort, and His encouragement. As I'd catch myself getting lost in my somber thoughts, it became easier to stop the tide of fear and regrets. My prayer life changed. Thanking Jesus for the countless daily gifts He continued to send my way, the burdens of the moments would lift.

All those months in bed, I listened to worship music, mainly the Brooklyn Tabernacle Choir. My friend Debby worked at a video store and brought me movies weekly. One woman cared for me weekly by washing and changing my bed linens for three months. Other girlfriends worked for Jim at the front desk of his dental office, refusing pay. Meals appeared every afternoon. When Jim's namesake uncle died in Michigan, a friend spent the weekend caring for me so he could attend the funeral. Someone always met Billy at the bus stop. Others would attend his daytime school talent shows, book fairs, and choral presentations, saying, "I'm here so I can tell your mom everything!" We were the recipient of help from family, friends, and strangers alike.

One thing I found terribly embarrassing was watching others do our dirty laundry. My friend had suffered a spinal cord injury years earlier and though handicapped, she was first to show up, digging into my dirty clothes hamper, and using the tray on her walker to transfer our stinky clothes into the washing machine. Nearly in tears, I begged her to stop and just visit with me. Her response was so profound.

"Look, I know how you feel. I've been where you are. Just remember, it's far easier to give a gift than it is to receive one. You need to be willing to let all of us be Jesus to you. Doing your laundry is my way of washing your feet."

Humility took on a whole new meaning.

Chapter 9

Understanding Us

Jeremiah 29:11-13–*"For I know the plans I have for you," declares the* LORD, *"plans to prosper you and not to harm you, plans to give you hope and a future. Then you will call on me and come and pray to me, and I will listen to you. You will seek me and find me when you seek me with all your heart."*

A fter four months, I could occasionally stomach solid foods. Terribly weak, I began to use my walker to leave the bedroom and join family and friends in the family room. My only therapy was walking waist deep in a pool for fifteen minutes daily. Jim held one arm and a friend grasped the other. Climbing out of the community pool created quite a ruckus from onlookers.

"Hey, can I help? Should I grab her foot and place it on the step? What happened? Car accident?"

Due to the agonizing, twenty-minute car ride to the nearest neighborhood pool, Jim took out a second mortgage on our home and had an in-ground, heated pool installed.

What began as a means of therapy reigned down benefits we could have never imagined. Owning a pool was enjoyable for our entire family. The summer season was extended due to our ability to heat the water. In addition to everyone in our family getting increased exercise, eventually, we hosted countless youth group events, birthday parties, neighborhood gatherings, and even Boy Scout canoe training in the deep end. It wasn't unusual for Jim to pull off his goggles after swimming laps to find a group of teens that had mysteriously appeared in the adjacent hot tub.

"Hi, Dr. Rhea! We counted and you did seventy-five laps."

Not everything in our lives was rosy, though. When Jim finally began to forgive himself for telling me to "hold on" that day in Mexico, I took up the mantel. Now that he felt better, I'd become quickly enraged when he would tell me what to do. Gripped by a new, underlying inability to forgive him, his comments infuriated me, triggering my old tendencies toward self-abuse. Bulimia resurfaced in a way I hadn't experienced in a decade. I'd become furious when Jim would suggest a practical suggestion.

"You pick up Billy after swim team and I'll mow."

After admitting my bulimia to a friend, she intervened by scheduling an appointment for me with a wise counselor. Reluctantly, I showed up. When the counselor asked about my marriage, I blurted out,

"He's such a jerk. If he hadn't told me to 'hold on,' I'd never be in this chronic pain. I'm so sick of him telling me what to do."

The moment she learned I had never admitted to him how angry I'd become, she said something very shocking to me.

"This week, Karen, you need to tell Jim about the anger you've been harboring and ask his forgiveness. He doesn't know what you're thinking and why you're snapping at him about insignificant things. Once you say it out loud, both of you can begin to heal."

Driving home from my appointment, I fumed at her inability to side with me. Believing all my emotions amounted to righteous anger, I began to pray through tears. Before pulling into my garage, my heart began to soften to her suggestion. That evening, after I asked Jim to forgive me for my years of mounting unforgiveness, we embraced – our tears mingling as they streamed down our cheeks. Her instructions were counter-intuitive to a secular psychologist's take on my predicament. She was right to hold me accountable. Unbeknownst to Jim, I was harboring resentment, inflaming the friction between us.

Following a mere three more sessions with my counselor, my head was screwed on straight and I benefited in ways I would have never imagined possible. Counseling no longer took place in her office. She became my dear friend; one of the wisest and wittiest women I've ever known. In fact, she and her husband joined our mutual friends for a monthly dinner and Bible study.

Jim and I did enter into a season of redefining our relationship. In addition to my physical disabilities, we had to deal with our son's mounting medical crisis. *Billy became desperately ill for six years, creating a grievous wedge between Jim and I that can only be described as an attack by the enemy. Yet, our marriage not only survived, it grew stronger.

*As told in Sick Kids And Those Who Love Them

It became apparent the Great Physician knew more than my physicians here on earth. I never lost bladder or bowel control. Constant pain ceased in an unexpected way due to surprising results following emergency surgery. Ten years after my accident, everything inside prolapsed outside. Talk about humiliating. Yet during surgery, it was discovered that my sigmoid and intestine were resting on a nerve trunk. Removed and sutured, I awoke from that operation totally aware that the constant stinging had disappeared. A true gift. Somewhere along the line, I stopped limping. During a test, my hips appeared perfectly level with no evidence of the previous three-quarter inch differential. There's simply no earthly explanation.

Psalm 118:8–*It is better to trust in the* LORD *than to put confidence in man.*

That Scripture remains the perfect explanation of why I'm able to hike, ride horses, downhill snow ski, and sit on an airplane. Vacuuming and climbing multiple steps kicks up my nerve damage. So I'm grateful for escalators and caring very little about my dirty floors.

It's been almost thirty years since my tumble off the cliff. I'm so thankful for kind, phenomenal doctors. I've endured multiple, gross medical tests, auto-immune issues, cervical fusions, aches and pains, and, yes, grey hair before I turned forty. The evening before my fall, villagers served us scrambled eggs. I haven't been able to stomach an egg since that day. That's no big deal, just interesting. Also, severe claustrophobia developed during my tenth MRI. Valium is my friend on such occasions.

When Jim entered his sixtieth decade, he faced back surgeries, a hip replacement, and a knee replacement. Roll reversal occurred and I became his caretaker. We'd often laugh when hearing young couples indicate that marriage is a fifty-fifty contract. Actually, it's a one hundred percent, all-embracing, sacrificial life together. For us, on the other side of difficult seasons, came a deeper intimacy and fuller joy.

There was one constant regardless of our circumstances. When Billy was born, we had begun praying together each morning. It's amazing how that one discipline cut through the frustrations, anger, and heartache that often crept into our marriage. Thanking Jesus daily for our blessings, praying for family and friend's needs, and asking for His forgiveness in the presence of one another brought healing into our home in a way that is indescribable.

Ecclesiastes 4:12 - *And though a man might prevail against one who is alone, two will withstand him—a threefold cord is not quickly broken.*

Not unlike Jim's words to me that day in Mexico, I think God has been telling me all these years to simply, "Hold on."

I've often thought about the moment my mule tumbled over that precipice. Maybe I was assigned an angel, not unlike Clarence in the Jimmy Stewart movie, "It's A Wonderful Life." When my heavenly Father yelled, "Go!" my angel swooped in and mistakenly caught the mule instead of me. Yes, everyone asks; the mule lived. Yet, I was spared as well. To God be the glory.

Jim & Karen with the family; Christmas 2016.
Top: Jim, Nicole, Maria, Billy, Lara, & Alan
Bottom: David, Erik, Jim, Karen, Jakob, & Kate

Chapter 10

Fifteen Minutes of Fame

Romans 1:16–*For I am not ashamed of the gospel, for it is the power of God for salvation to everyone who believes, to the Jew first and also to the Greek.*

Karen, Jim and Billy Rhea were filmed last November for an episode of "Rescue 911" that will air Tuesday at 8 p.m. on WUSA-TV Channel 9. The episode reenacts a February 1992 incident when Karen Rhea fell off a cliff in Mexico.

Local family to appear on Rescue 911

T he television docudrama "Rescue 911" received word of my accident and rescue. The following year, 1993, the show's producers contacted Jim. They felt my accident and rescue would make for great television drama. Billy and Jim were offered an all-expense paid trip to Oaxaca, Mexico to star as themselves in the story of my accident. Producers tried to dissuade me from accompanying them, feeling I'd be a liability. Even though a stunt woman was hired to reenact my fall, I wasn't about to let my little boy return to the jungles without me. Yes, I was plagued with nerve damage in my lower back. But, I felt a supply of narcotics would get me though the travel. I had rarely taken any drugs before my fall down the cliff, not even aspirin. Learning to live with pain had become a new way of life. If things became too hard on location, I would remain in my hotel room on any given day.

We had so much to consider. Even though there would be no financial compensation for our family, it would be an incredible story to share with viewers. We speculated how a national television program, in primetime, would reenact the old man giving Jim his horse and miraculously reappearing at the river bank, while emphasizing the sacrificial service of the Indians rescuing us, the power of prayer, and God's grace through it all. Two bonuses sweetened the pot: we would meet Dr. Garcia once again, and Jim would be given time to provide dental care in the village that helped us the previous year. At my insistence, producers agreed to let me tag along. The filming took place November 1993, just three months shy of the two-year anniversary of my accident.

Rescue 911 crew sets up equipment in the Rhea's kitchen for interviews.

The director prepares to interview Billy.

The Hollywood crew arrived at our home to interview us for an accurate storyline. The director knew how to invoke tears by poignant questions.

"So Jim, Karen's bleeding to death and it's your fault. What were you thoughts while you waited all those hours for help?"

Billy thought the interview was fun. He was not easily troubled; instead, his personality was revealed the minute the camera started to roll. Without any prompting, he stated,

"When we left the village, it was sort of like a long dirt road, no jungle on either side. The trail was about two iguanas wide."

After our interviews ended and lunch was delivered to our house, they followed us around to try and make us look interesting in our day-to-day routine. Then the crew left to interview my orthopedist as an expert witness to my injuries.

During that season of life, I was singing with the National Christian Choir, so Hollywood stepped in and filmed our Monday night choral rehearsal. I think we sang "Amazing Grace" two dozen times. Knowing a film crew was coming, everyone seemed to have taken extra time in front of their mirrors. We all got a kick out of the experience.

The following day, Jim, Billy, and I flew to Mexico and settled in our hotel. A meeting was scheduled in the director's room across the parking lot. As Billy chattered excitedly, speculating about what was in store, Jim elbowed me.

"How weird is this? If you weren't beside me, I'd think you were right in front of me."

Walking toward me was my stunt double, Marian. Smiling broadly, she pointed directly at me, then back at her face. We all had a good laugh. Hollywood did a good job finding a look-alike; she resembled my first cousin.

The first order of business would take place that very afternoon. While Billy and I rested up in our hotel room, Jim took the film crew into areas of the jungle to identify similar terrain where my accident occurred. The actual location of my fall was too remote for filming.

My stunt double confessed her expertise was falling off buildings and cliffs, not riding burros.

The Mexico City film crew was also involved, hiring extras and even the actors and actresses playing parts of the missionaries and dental support team. Filming got behind because the actor playing the missionary showed up drunk two days in a row. He couldn't even hold his head up. The most comical event occurred when the actress playing Flo, the missionary's wife, drove a station wagon like a bat out of hell up to the airplane, clipping its wing, not once but twice. I stood back and listened to everyone screaming profanities in English and Spanish.

"Stop, stop, holy _ _ _ _! She's gonna hit it again!"

Each day provided memorable moments. The following evening, the director called us into his hotel room. Shots of tequila were being consumed by his colleagues to possibly numb their physical aches and pains following long, ten-hour work days. The atmosphere in the room and downtrodden expressions on everyone's faces negated a party-like aura.

"You want to talk job stress? Check out the mule the Mexico City film crew proudly dropped off in my room for tomorrow's shoot. It resembles a piñata."

Just in case the real mule didn't cooperate, a substitute was provided. This was not up to the standards our Hollywood filmmaking professionals were accustomed. The following day, the film crew stood the piñata containing no candy beside a real mule. The live mule kicked it over. Those scenes were cut.

Billy posing with the fake mule.

*Resting on my make-shift stretcher, a Les Miserable T-Shirt
seems suitable.*

Marian Green, my stunt double, was hardworking and
eased my mind throughout filming. I couldn't have asked for
a better buddy. Watching her work her craft was an education.
She threw herself backwards off a ten foot cliff onto open, card-
board boxes, duplicating my fall for the camera crew. After
knocking the wind out of herself, she was instructed to climb
the hill again for another take because the corner of the box
appeared in the shot. Without hesitation, she shot me a smile,
giving a thumbs up and climbed back up the cliff for a retake.
Marian went on to not only perform stunts in her risky line of
work, but also coordinate stunts for feature films and in 2013
received the Helen Gibson Award at the Action Icon Awards.

R.A. Rondell was the stunt coordinator for our story. Billy
and I loved riding in the jeep with him to our daily locations, as
he was a masterful story teller and gave us the inside scoop on
many actors. R.A.'s entire family was in the business. His dad

had been Steve McQueen's stunt double, which I knew would thrill my mom. In the final scene of "Jurassic Park," R.A. can be seen hanging from the dinosaur bones. He became the stunt coordinator for dozens of well-known blockbusters movies.

The following years, our family was the last to leave movie theaters as we watched the credits roll, hoping to catch a glimpse of R.A. or Marian's names. Workers waited patiently to clean up candy wrappers and popcorn until one of the three of us scream,

"There! There's R.A.!"

Hanging out with professionals and watching them in action was a highlight. Naively, little did we know we'd have no input as to what would be left on the cutting room floor. Also, the elements were just as taxing in November as they were in February, the previous year. The one exception was that we did have caterers for every meal. That was terribly embarrassing, as the desperately poor looked longingly from a distance as aromas wafted into their villages. We were forbidden to share.

Following a few days of filming, Jim and I set up his dental clinic in a village. During the work day, Billy handed out bags of toothbrushes, toothpaste, and toys. Even though this day was an unplanned shoot, the camera man began filming Jim working, as the crew stepped up to help by cleaning instruments and keeping patients seated after being injected. For me, personally that was the best day, as I felt Jim was able to accomplish more than he'd hoped. Not only did he relieve his patients' pain, but his selflessness touched onlookers in a surprising, significant way.

The most difficult part of the trip was due to my vivid recollections from the previous year. Flashbacks began immediately when roosters crowed before sunrise the morning of our arrival. In our hotel room, just before fully waking, my pain was reminiscent of those days in the clinic. Breathing into a bag to prevent hyperventilating became my typical morning routine.

When Jim wasn't being filmed, he recorded the crew at work with our movie camera from home. When he was to appear in a scene, he'd hand it to me for safe keeping or to film when they'd yell, "Action!" One of the stranger occurrences happened as I was filming the scene where my stunt-double's head was in Jim's lap after reenacting my fall. Looking through the lens of my large movie camera mimicked the boxy, fragmented views of the world while in shock. Who knew it would flood back those recollections so vividly? In seconds, I had a flawless memory of the event.

"Stop filming! Billy, you were standing over there. Bob was there and the others stood behind Billy."

When the filming went on days longer than originally planned, Jim said he had to get back to his patients at home. He was offered a substantial amount of money to stay. When he declined, the producer became noticeably irritated. She could not fathom his work ethic over monetary gain. That afternoon, her husband was going up in an airplane, strapped on the side of the wing to film overhead shots for the program. As the engine reeved up, I yelled,

"Enjoy!"

Frustrated with Jim, and now likely cross with me too, she snapped,

"You have no idea how dangerous this is!"

The director grabbed her and said,

"Have you lost your mind? Do you know who you're talking to? I think she actually does know how dangerous it is down here."

Despite the stress, everyone was kind to our boy. Yet his observations and new experiences clouded any enjoyment as

77

the days dragged on. During those two weeks, B's legs, arms, and face were covered in bug bites. The miserable heat added to the boredom of filmmaking.

"Take ten!"

Our little guy also had to witness the mistreatment of the mule. After filming Marian's tumble off the mountain, the hope was to show the mule after the fall, laying down, then jumping up and running off. Our director pulled their director aside, explaining how the American public would need to see the mule survive the fall or PETA would be down their throats. The Mexican film crew was unsuccessful trying to coax him to perform. He'd either hee-haw and buck or lay down and simply not move. Hence, stubborn as a mule. Etched in my mind is the horrified look on B's face, as locals attempted to beat the mule with a crop into submission. It never worked.

The final day of filming, the director told us that our son was a natural on film and because he had several speaking parts, he could be granted his Screen Actors Guild card. We suggested he run the offer by our son. I was so excited, thinking of my little actor and the Academy Awards I'd get to attend in his honor. At lunch, when the offer was presented, Bill responded,

"No, thank you."

Next he was asked,

"Well, what do you want to do when you grow up?"

Bill's blue eyes narrowed and with a stern response, after being traumatized by the treatment of the mules,

"I'm considering going into animal welfare."

It really was time to go home.

A year later, the three of us sat in front of the TV to watch our episode of "Rescue 911." All in all, the finished production was pretty good. There were a few disappointments. Jim was a huge "Star Trek" fan and had watched all the series' episodes. Being a 'Trekkie," having the host, William Shatner, introduce him by name was a rip. But the excitement quickly deflated when Shatner said, "Maryland dentist Jim Rhea was on a 'goodwill mission.'" Apparently, the accuracy of saying "A Christian mission" ruffled someone's feathers. To me, it was such a shame they cut Jim providing dental work at the village. Also, the cutting room floor sweepings included the old man giving Jim the reins of his horse. Jim is shown limping alone as he narrates,

"I couldn't keep up and was falling further and further behind."

The storyline was left hanging out there and they switched back to my rescuers.

Also upsetting to me was the fact that the story indicated I fell off the mule instead of specifying it was the mule that fell off that twenty-five foot cliff with me on his back. How embarrassing for me, as it made me appear klutzy. Yet I had to recall the mule's inability to act.

My orthopedist's interview was cut. He telephoned afterwards to tell me he and his wife held a huge party to watch the show. The minute he heard Billy say, "The doctor from Veracruz didn't charge us anything" he laughingly knew he was sliced out of the program. How disappointing, as I loved and respected Dr. Goral.

On the whole, though, our story was well documented. The Indians praying over me and our faith were clearly depicted. My choir was highlighted. Jim, Billy, and I experienced raw emotion at different moments of the show. One segment was unexpected for all of us. While being interviewed at our house, they filmed us outside with our horses and dogs. At the conclusion of our fifteen minutes of fame, cameras zoomed in on our Irish Setter, Rusty, barking and wagging his tail. In 1983,

Jim and I picked him up from the animal shelter before Billy was born. He had just died weeks before the show aired. B commented,

"That was the best part of the show. I really miss Rusty."

"Rescue 911" captured our real life in so many ways.

Many years later, Jim was providing dental care in Hyderabad, India. One evening, he was visiting with his host family. Behind him, a television was turned on, but the volume was low so everyone could visit. Suddenly, ten guests and the host family were glancing back and forth at the screen and Jim. Someone exclaimed,

"Turn it up! Turn it up! Dr. Jim, isn't that you?"

Sure enough, the cancelled show, "Rescue 911," was re-airing our program in this third-world area, Indian Runner Rescue from 1994. Laughing, Jim exclaimed,

"Yep. That's me. I've been reduced to a rerun."

Our son, Bill, is a man of deep faith and conviction, and possesses a dry wit. Inheriting a love for literature from his dad, my gene for entertaining, and a deep gratification surrounded by friends was passed on as well. He and his wife Maria, an endocrinologist, were married in 2012. They are active in their church. Bill was awarded his master's degree in St. Louis, is now an adjunct professor, manages his Airbnb, and sings with the San Antonio Choral Society. Recently, he returned to Africa for his third mission trip. His dad's influence is unmistakable.

My accident in Mexico, coupled with other life-altering events, have allowed me to encourage others facing their own trials. What a blessing to have family and friends who pray for me daily and encourage me to tell my story publicly. The gift of longevity has helped me discover God's amazing grace in and beyond my valleys of despair. Without a doubt, I've experienced the thrill of mountaintop moments in abundance. Yet,

I'm especially grateful for seasons of tranquility where I'm able to stroll through fields of green, placid meadows. It is in those pastures where I deeply sense the tenderness of my Shepherd's love. How true it is that mountaintops inspire us. But the valleys mature us. Both are necessary in life. Jesus never fails to renew my hope and joy.

Epilogue

Jim & Karen

My husband was a man of integrity and wit, seeking out adventure one moment, yet easily slowing down to enjoy a good book or experiencing solitude in nature. He loved deeply

82

and was deeply loved, living a service-filled sixty-nine years. It wasn't always easy for him, the kids, or me as he battled depression and all that comes with it his entire adult life. He is now free indeed after succumbing to pancreatic cancer June 23, 2018.

The following year, I sold our home in Boyds, Maryland. Settling temporarily in our vacation home in Stanardsville, Virginia, I found it incredibly cathartic to work on my manuscript, sitting at Jim's desk where he wrote his own memoir trilogy, "I Swear To Tell the Tooth, The Whole Tooth, And Nothing But The Tooth" under the pseudonym Dr. Carroll James. My inherited office overlooks the Piedmont Valley and the Blue Ridge Mountains. It's a divine spot to work through my grief and reminisce, all while witnessing early morning sunrises as I ruminate on God's creation.

Life truly is short at its longest and I miss him with all my heart. My comfort remains steeped in the blessed assurance that his eternal residence in heaven is secure— not because he was a good man, which he was, but because of his deep and abiding faith in Jesus Christ.

Boyds Presbyterian Church Cemetery, Boyds, Maryland